This book is dedicated to you, the reade
wish that as you read each page you wil
closer to you. So come, start each day w
with God and may your heart soon be
peace.

Compiled by: Helen Lesman

Cover by: Janet ANDERSON
                (a talented, dear frienc

Heart to Heart. Copyright © 1988, 1991
LIGHTEN UP ENTERPRISES
5223 Edina Industrial Boulevard
Edina, MN 55439-2910

HOW TO BE HAPPY ALL THROUGH THE YEAR

Keep your heart free from hate,
Your mind free from worry.
Live simply, expect little,
Give much, sing often, pray always,
Fill your life with love, scatter sunshine,
Forget self, think of others.
Do as you would be done by.
These are the tried links
In contentment's golden chain.

JANUARY 1

Thank You, Dear Lord, for watching over me all the year through. Keep me close to You all through the coming year too. Watch over my friends and loved ones and I pray that we will all be together for yet another year. Amen

DECEMBER 31

Let my words and the meditation of my heart be acceptable to Thee all this day, O Lord, my strength and my redeemer. Amen

Last year I made a list of things
That I resolved to do;
I'll use that list again this year,
It's still as good as new!

JANUARY 2

Dear Lord, I often say I forgive, but keep the hostilities shut up within. Beginning with me, start a chain reaction of forgiving love. Amen

Practice makes perfect except when it comes to getting up in the morning.

DECEMBER 30

Father, when I grieve, thank You for Your comfort amid my sorrow. Help me to make my grief bearable to myself and my loved ones. Amen

People are certainly peculiar — they want the front of the bus, the back of the church and the middle of the road.

JANUARY 3

O Lord, help me to recognize and use opportunities that come my way — opportunities to help others as well as myself. Amen

Why is it listeners always know when
the speaker should stop and
he seldom does?

DECEMBER 29

As I ask for Your forgiveness and embrace it, give me the courage to extend a forgiving hand to those who have hurt me. Amen

Flattery is the art of telling another person exactly what he thinks of himself.

JANUARY 4

O Lord, give me the courage to stand for something. Let me not be content to wait and see what will happen but give me the determination to make the right things happen. Amen

How come vices are more habit forming than virtues?

DECEMBER 28

Teach me not to make light of the sufferings of others. Grant me understanding and compassion for those who are less fortunate than I. Amen

Burn the candle at both ends and you douhle the chances of getting your fingers burned.

JANUARY 5

Dear Lord, teach me to make my prayers more meaningful and sincere. So often I find myself praying mechanically and I know this is not the way to talk to You. Amen

Some speakers need no introduction,
they just need a conclusion.

DECEMBER 27

Dear Lord, please don't give up on me. I know that it is through me that Thy will be done — help me to see Your way. Amen

One thing I've learned in growing old
No doubt you've noticed too:
The kids to whom you gave advice
Now give advice to you.

JANUARY 6

When I am afraid Lord, it means I have strayed away from Your teachings. Grasp my outstretched hand and keep me close to Your heart. Amen

Why is it that a minute contains 60 seconds except when it's preceded by "Just a"?

DECEMBER 26

Father, quiet my mind so that I may hear Your words that will give me peace. Let me feel your nearness and love. Amen

The trouble with the younger generation is that it hasn't read the minutes of the last meeting.

JANUARY 7

CHRISTMAS

We will not "spend" Christmas
Nor "observe" Christmas
But we will "keep" Christmas.
Keep it
as it is in all the loveliness
of its ancient traditions.
May we keep it in our hearts
that we may keep
in its hope.

DECEMBER 25

Dear Lord, when Your children are in need, may I be the one to help by caring and sharing. Amen

A politician is someone who never met
a tax he didn't hike.

JANUARY 8

O God — Open all our hearts
To the wonderful spirit
In the world tonight;
Not just on Christmas,
But every day.
What a joyous place
Our earth would be
If only we would keep Christmas
The whole year through.

Author Unknown

DECEMBER 24

Dear Father, keep me from developing grandiose opinions of myself. Help me to remember I am not infallible and that You love all Your children the same. Amen

There is nothing like sealing a letter to inspire a fresh thought.

JANUARY 9

God is with me and I am with God. God's blessings of life, light and love flow through me. I have a special place in God's world. Amen

Christmas shoppers are people with
the spirit of brotherly shove.

DECEMBER 23

Forgive me Lord when I hurt other people, prod me to look hard at myself and be less critical of those around me. Amen

Seeing ourselves as others see us wouldn't do any good. We wouldn't believe it.

JANUARY 10

O Lord, You have brought me to this new day and further opportunity. Help me to work with You so that it may be a good day with good things done. Amen

Ever notice how hard it is to keep your head when your neck is on the line?

DECEMBER 22

Eternal God, instill in me the desire to be understanding and supportive of those with whom I disagree. Help me to remember we do not have to agree in all things to live in harmony. Amen

Anybody can grab a tiger by the tail.
You only survive by knowing
what to do next.

JANUARY 11

Holy Father, soften my heart and tongue when anger has overtaken me. Teach me how to be forgiving toward those who hurt me. Amen

Some of us are on a rotation diet of our own. Every time we turn around, we eat.

DECEMBER 21

Lord, I'd like to think that mine is the perfect church. Open my mind to those who think differently and help me to accept that You love everyone of us in the same way. Amen

The big fish always gets away — that's why they're big.

JANUARY 12

All my needs rest in Your care, dear Lord, for which I offer You thanksgiving and praise, now and forever. Amen

Some people eat from the three
basic food groups —
canned, frozen and take-out.

DECEMBER 20

Heavenly Father, watch over my loved ones today. Comfort them when they fail, rejoice with them when they succeed. Be Thou their vision. Amen

If water pollution gets any worse,
walking on it will be a cinch.

JANUARY 13

Dear Lord, may I grasp the opportunity to be kind to someone today — and then to another. Amen

Success is not what you gain in life or accomplish for yourself. It's what you do for others.

DECEMBER 19

Lord, I thank You for life. May I be sensitive to everyone's needs and ambitions and be a supportive pillar. Amen

Why are the godless everywhere
So frightened by the sound of prayer?

JANUARY 14

When I am in the shadows, dear Lord, help me to trust and not be afraid. I know You will not forsake me. Amen

Remember when "enter" was a sign on a door and not a button on a computer?

DECEMBER 18

Father in heaven, sometimes I am easily discouraged. When that happens I need to be reminded that You care and are with me now and forever. Amen

The last word in an argument is what a wife says. Anything a husband says after that, is the beginning of another argument.

JANUARY 15

O God, thank You for the difference You are making in my life. Keep me strong in the belief that absolutely nothing can defeat Your love. Amen

Remember when TV bloopers were a rare mistake — not the entire show?

DECEMBER 17

Dear Lord, restore me to the joy of Your saving grace and put a new and optimistic spirit within me. Amen

If at first you do succeed, it's too easy
— try something else.

JANUARY 16

O Lord, I thank You for the gift of this challenging life. Let me have the confidence that wherever it leads me, I am only following You. Amen

Some books are not to be tossed aside lightly. They should be thrown with emphatic force.

DECEMBER 16

O Father, when I walk in darkness, show me Your great light. Be my strength and my salvation. Amen

Disneyland is the greatest people trap
ever built by a mouse.

JANUARY 17

O God, help me to understand that it is only by serving others in Your name that we find love, peace and joy in our faith. Amen

Confession is good for the soul — and sometimes royalties.

DECEMBER 15

Dear Lord, there are so many who cry out for help. I know I cannot help them all, so guide me to the most helpless and to give without expecting a reward. Amen

Poverty is no disgrace —
it's just inconvenient.

JANUARY 18

In my heart I know that God is with me,
that God loves me, that God never fails me,
so my heart has every reason to smile. Amen

Holding on to anger is like grasping a
hot coal with the intent of throwing it at
someone — you are the one
who gets burned.

DECEMBER 14

You light the way Lord, and I ask for Your understanding and forgiveness when I stray from the path You set before me. Amen

It's not enough for a gardener to love flowers. He must also hate weeds.

JANUARY 19

Help me Lord, to do Your work even when I find it unappealing and difficult. Amen

If everything seems to be coming your way, you're probably in the wrong lane.

DECEMBER 13

O God, You are the source of my comfort. Walk with me this day and give me strength to bear my burdens. With You beside me I will endure all things. Amen

The man who claims he never made a mistake in his life generally has a wife who did.

JANUARY 20

Dear God, I am well aware that I can't make it on my own. So take my hand and hold it tight, for I can't walk alone. Amen

I am not young enough
to know everything.

DECEMBER 12

Sometimes, Dear Lord, my days get so busy I forget about You. I am ever thankful You do not forget about me. Amen

The world is divided into good people
and bad people and the good people
decide which is which.

JANUARY 21

Dear Lord, when I am hungry for faith and feel lost and lonely with doubt, help me to find my way to You. Amen

How about an undeclared peace?

DECEMBER 11

When life seems to be overwhelming, God, help me to subdue my frustrations and feel your quieting, loving hand on my shoulder. Amen

One of the pleasures of age is looking
back at the girls you didn't marry.

JANUARY 22

Loving God, Your wisdom is mine to use if only I would take the time to read and listen to Your word. May I learn to live as the scriptures teach. Amen

The best thing to hold onto in this world is each other.

DECEMBER 10

Merciful Lord, remind me that You are in control and that when I leave things in Your hands my burdens are lighter. Amen

Good judgment comes from experience — usually experience which was the result of poor judgment.

JANUARY 23

O God, I need help to understand that faith is not a blind acceptance but a certain reasonable knowledge. Amen

Always remember that you are absolutely unique — just like everyone else.

DECEMBER 9

Father in heaven, I sometimes forget to thank You for Your generous blessings. Remind me they are not mine to keep, but to be shared with those who struggle with less. Amen

Conceit is an odd disease; it makes everyone sick but the one who has it.

JANUARY 24

Dear Father, I will try to look forward to the changes in my life without fear. I know You will lead me safely through every path. Amen

Behind every successful man is a
surprised father-in-law.

DECEMBER 8

Dear Lord, I know You are not a cruel, punishing God, so when things go wrong keep me from blaming you and help me to accept my responsibilities. Amen

Even when a marriage is made in heaven, the maintenance work has to be done here on earth.

JANUARY 25

I pray, O Lord, that I will set aside my wants for this day and make it a better day for someone else. Amen

A speech, to be immortal, does not have to be eternal.

DECEMBER 7

Father, teach me to trust in You and to leave things in Your hands. Instill in me the confidence that You love me now and always. Amen

A man can usually tell what kind of a time he's having at a party by the look on his wife's face.

JANUARY 26

Bless my family today, Lord, and bring us closer together if not in body then in Spirit. We need each other and You beside us. Amen

Pain is forgotten; insult lingers on.

DECEMBER 6

Father, loving parent of all of us, when I experience loneliness, with no sense of Your presence, speak to me, open my heart to Your Spirit within me. Amen

Some women are looking for a man
who is tall, dark and has some.

JANUARY 27

Dear Lord, Help me to find You when I search for You. Sometimes I forget You are the hope reaching out to all of us. Amen

We are the people our parents
warned us against.

DECEMBER 5

Dear Father, sometimes I am preoccupied with the troublesome details of my life. Help me to see beyond the temporary and focus on Your brighter promise. Amen

A good wife laughs at her husband's jokes, not because they are clever, but because she is.

JANUARY 28

Dear Father, help me to remember to tell those who help me how much I appreciate their efforts and services. May I never take kindness for granted. Amen

Never argue with a fool — people might not know the difference.

DECEMBER 4

Heavenly Father, lift me from my complacency. Make me do more than be aware of those who suffer, those who are hungry, those who are ill. Arouse in me a helpful spirit. Amen

Be careful of your thoughts; They may break into words at any time.

JANUARY 29

Sometimes I lose my way God. Strengthen my wavering spirit and bring me close to You when I stray from the path to You. Amen

Friends may come and go, but enemies accumulate.

DECEMBER 3

Dear Lord, sometimes I need help relating to other people. Sometimes I judge others needlessly. Forgive me and work your power of love within me. Amen

You can accomplish anything if you have patience. You can even carry water in a sieve — if you wait until it freezes.

JANUARY 30

God of all creation, help me to see You in all of life, that I may never know a moment without Your presence. Amen

The man who can smile when things go wrong has thought of someone he can blame it on.

DECEMBER 2

Lead me to the path where I should go, Precious Lord. Show me the right road for me to walk. I have no hope except in You. Amen

The end never really justifies the meanness.

JANUARY 31

Dear Lord, forgive me when I presume upon Your mercy and patience. Create in me this day a heart that desires only to please Thee. Amen

God knows us better than we know ourselves and He loves us better too.

DECEMBER 1

Father in Heaven, remind me this day that I am your means of justice. Prod me to do the good things and help create an atmosphere that would please You. Amen

A swap is a trade between two people who think they skinned each other.

FEBRUARY 1

Dear Lord, should I feel troubled today, help me to remember that You are always near with comforting arms. Amen

Take care that the face which looks out from your mirror each morning is a pleasant face. You may not see it again all day, but others will.

NOVEMBER 30

I shall live in the light of God. It guides me and shines through me. My mind and my heart are open to love and forgiveness. Amen

You can always tell a well informed man — his views are the same as yours.

FEBRUARY 2

May I have patience all this day with my friends, fellow workers and family. In this I need Your help, dear Lord. Amen

When the outlook is poor,
try the uplook.

NOVEMBER 29

Whenever I seek God in all that I do, I am amazed at the wondrous ways in which God works. Amen

Money may not be everything, but it is
a great consolation until
you have everything.

FEBRUARY 3

God satisfies my longing soul and fills my life with His good. I am richly blessed. I trust the Spirit of God in myself and in my loved ones. Amen

Taxes could be worse — suppose we had to pay on what we think we're worth.

NOVEMBER 28

Lord, sometimes I feel I have a right to complain, but I do not want my life to become saturated with negative feelings. Help me to turn toward the positive. Amen

When most people are caught between
two evils, most take the one
they've never tried.

FEBRUARY 4

Oh Lord, now that I have tasted the sweetness of Your love, my selfish desires no longer have power. Thank You for loving me. Amen

Funny how a dollar can look so big when you take it to church, and so small when you take it to the store.

NOVEMBER 27

Dear Lord, awaken me to what I am and help me become the most I can be for Thee. Amen

An honest politician is one who when he is bought will stay bought.

FEBRUARY 5

Dear Father, when I center my life around You, I am filled with vitality. You have given my life completeness. Amen

History keeps repeating itself because
we weren't listening the first time.

NOVEMBER 26

O Father, there are times when I am wrapped in self-pity. Take my hand and show me those who are truly suffering and fill me with a desire to ease their pain. Amen

Then there was a fellow who discovered a way to hammer nails without hitting his thumb. He had his wife hold the nails.

FEBRUARY 6

I am grateful, dear Lord, for Your not giving up on me. I know You are constantly at work in me, remolding me into the image You have planned for me. Amen

Lots of men need two women; a secretary to take everything down and a wife to pick everything up.

NOVEMBER 25

No man can truthfully declare: I don't need God, I don't need prayer. There are times when, weary of walking alone, we need strength beyond our own. Amen

Love does not consist of two people looking at each other, but of two people looking in the same direction.

FEBRUARY 7

Heavenly Father, thank You for patiently teaching me the meaning of faith and hope. Though I am slowly learning to trust You completely, You do not turn away from me. Amen

Strange how some people would like
to abolish prayer just
when the country
needs it most.

NOVEMBER 24

Dear Lord, help me to right the wrongs in my life; to accept what I cannot change and then turn toward the positive. Amen

There is nothing wrong in having
nothing to say — unless you
insist on saying it.

FEBRUARY 8

Precious Lord — *Instill in me that with Your help I can handle or change situations. Give me the trust to believe You will always be there to help me conquer my fears. Amen*

Did you ever get the feeling that
perhaps your gray hair isn't premature?

NOVEMBER 23

O God, I know I am not perfect and You know I am not perfect. I ask that You help me grow in the direction that pleases you and leave all my regrets behind. Amen

The worst thing about growing old is
having to listen to a lot of advice
from one's children.

FEBRUARY 9

Dear Lord, how patiently You teach me the meaning of faith and hope. Forgive me if I am slow to trust You completely. Amen

If the knocking at the door is unusually loud and long, it isn't opportunity — it's relatives.

NOVEMBER 22

In my mind, Dear Lord, I know there are a great many people in real trouble. Now open my heart and direct my steps to them with understanding and outstretched arms. Amen

A class reunion is when everyone gets together to see who is falling apart.

FEBRUARY 10

Almighty God, my heart overflows with gratitude for all Thy blessings. I pray that I shall always be worthy of Your great love. Amen

Today it isn't facing the music that hurts, it's listening to it.

NOVEMBER 21

O Lord, I have so many faults. I try to be aware of them and reform my ways, but often fall back. Help me to see myself as others see me and grant me the determination to change. Amen

You've reached middle-age when all you exercise is caution.

FEBRUARY 11

Father, You have given me the ability to make choices. Now I call on You to help me make the right choices. Amen

Save for a rainy day and a new tax comes along and soaks you.

NOVEMBER 20

Dear Father, open my heart and close my lips and let me exalt You in silent reverence this day. Amen

By the time a man realizes that maybe his father was right, he usually has a son who thinks he's wrong.

FEBRUARY 12

Dear Lord, with Your help I have been released from grief and pain. With You beside me, I am able to function with peace in my heart. Amen

Always keep your head up but be
careful to keep your nose
at a friendly level.

NOVEMBER 19

Lord, I've been cross and impatient. Help me to remember that in order to be loved, I must be loveable. Amen

There is more to life than
increasing its speed.
Mahatma Gandhi

FEBRUARY 13

Oh Lord, I pray for those who need to be comforted and uplifted. Bless them and keep them close to Your heart. Amen

A diplomat is someone who can disagree without being disagreeable.

NOVEMBER 18

Dear Lord, if I am too busy today to listen to you, please do not be too busy to watch over me. Amen

There is no cure for birth and death, so why not enjoy the interval.

FEBRUARY 14

Heavenly Father, You look inside my heart and know my concerns and hopes. Make me aware of the needs of those around me and instill in me the compassion and desire to help those who need help. Amen

Some folks are so busy being good
they forget they should be
busy doing good.

NOVEMBER 17

Father, I am often blind to your blessings. Remind me that you are at work within me and around me; that I need only to unlock my heart to You to receive Your blessings. Amen

A vegetarian is a person who won't
eat anything that
can have children.

FEBRUARY 15

Dear Lord, thank You for another new day — may I live it with faith and joy in my heart. Extend my hand to those who are hurting. Amen

A reckless driver is one who passes you on the highway in spite of all your car can do.

NOVEMBER 16

I need the true generosity of spirit, Dear God, so that when other people succeed, I can be genuinely glad and show it sincerely. Amen

Some people don't hesitate to speak
their mind because they have
nothing to lose.

FEBRUARY 16

Loving God, I pray for the understanding to forgive those who have hurt me. Open my heart to be forgiving as You have so often forgiven me. Amen

For fixing things around the house nothing beats a man who's handy with a checkbook.

NOVEMBER 15

Father, deep within me is my determination, my strength, my will to survive. It comes from You and I thank You. Amen

Only the mediocre are at their best.

FEBRUARY 17

Father, let this day be a day of unselfish service to You and to those around me. Amen

Time flies, but remember, you
are the navigator.

NOVEMBER 14

Lord, I pray for the courage of my convictions. Instill in me the determination to make the right things happen. Amen

The difference between genius and
stupidity is that genius has its limits.

FEBRUARY 18

Dear Lord, if love and concern for those around me is a disease, let me be a carrier. Not just for today, but every day. Amen

Why not go out on the limb? That's where all the fruit is.

NOVEMBER 13

Heavenly Father, with You I have the strength to overcome all things. I close my eyes, I feel Your presence and I am filled with hope. Amen

As you travel through life, leave your mark, not a stain.

FEBRUARY 19

God, Protector of us all, teach me and my loved ones to live unafraid in this world of violence. Protect us I pray. Amen

Some people think they are generous because they give away free advice.

NOVEMBER 12

Dear Lord, I know You hear me when I pray. Help me to hear You so that I may know Your will and live in obedience to it with love and joy. Amen

A successful executive in business is one who can delegate all the responsibility, shift all the blame, and appropriate all the credit.

FEBRUARY 20

Dear Father, stand beside me and help me to accept from Your hand the sweet and the bitter, the joy and the sorrow which enters into all our lives. Amen

God loves you; pass it along.

NOVEMBER 11

Father in Heaven, I often forget how fortunate I am that I have family and friends that love me. Help me to remember how empty my life would be without them. Amen

Some of us used to dream of the day we might be earning the salary we're struggling on now.

FEBRUARY 21

My heart sings with gratitude, Dear Lord, for Thy generosity to me and to my loved ones. Our lives are full. May we happily share with those who have so much less. Amen

If faith can see every step of the way,
it isn't faith.

NOVEMBER 10

The truest test of friendship is to sincerely share someone's joy and accomplishment without a trace of envy. Help me to be that kind of friend, Dear Lord. Amen

The best way to appreciate your job is
to imagine yourself without one.

FEBRUARY 22

Just for today, Lord, I will live through the next 12 hours and try not to tackle all of life's problems at once. Amen

Too many folks go through life running from something that isn't after them.

NOVEMBER 9

Dear Lord, when I set goals give me the courage to reach higher than I think possible. Fill me with confidence that with You beside me all things are possible. Amen

Something is wrong when the packaging is more durable than the product enclosed.

FEBRUARY 23

Father, sometimes I feel self-righteous because I faithfully go to church and pray to You. I need to remember that You love all Your children the same. Amen

When you help someone up a hill,
you're that much nearer
the top yourself.

NOVEMBER 8

Father, I often say that I forgive but still keep resentment within me. Starting with me, let me begin a chain reaction of forgiving love. Amen

If you want something done, give it to a busy man — and he'll have his secretary do it.

FEBRUARY 24

Father in Heaven, bless me and heal me of every prejudice, every jealousy and every envy. Thank You for Your loving care. Amen

A person's age can be measured by the degree of pain one feels as one comes in contact with a new idea.

NOVEMBER 7

Father in Heaven, Give me strength to be a Christian in everything I do and say, when it is much easier to be otherwise. Amen

Choose a job you love and you'll never have to work a day in your life.

Confucius

FEBRUARY 25

O Lord, thank You for finding me when I feel lost and drawing me closer into the circle of Your love. Amen

One way to end wars is to make the universal minimum draft age sixty.

NOVEMBER 6

Dear Lord, guard my loved ones as they work their way through another day. Lift their spirits when they feel discouraged and bring them home safely. Amen

Let us be thankful for fools; but for them the rest of us could not succeed.

FEBRUARY 26

I pray for Your Spirit of understanding to fill my heart when I have been offended. Let me start this day with a renewed mind. Amen

How long a minute is, depends on which side of the bathroom door you're on.

NOVEMBER 5

Heavenly Father, give me the will power to stop buying things I really don't need. I often feel deserving of a special purchase and then I worry about paying for it. Help me to put my needs and wants in proper perspective. Amen

The chicken probably came before the egg because it's hard to imagine God wanting to sit on an egg.

FEBRUARY 27

Father, I need to stop whatever I am doing at this moment and remember that I am loved by You as if I were Your only child. Thank You for that steadfast love. Amen

What is a cynic? Someone who knows
the price of everything and
the value of nothing.

NOVEMBER 4

Dear Lord, I am often filled with regrets and resentments. Help me to let go of those unpleasant memories and instead to look to the future with happy anticipation. Amen

Living with a saint is more grueling than being one.

FEBRUARY 28

I am grateful Lord, for the people who brighten my day with laughter. Help me do the same for others. Amen

If you're pushing fifty,
that's exercise enough.

NOVEMBER 3

Gracious God, help me to do my work with gladness. May I use the talents You gave me to do positive things today. Amen

Triumph is just "umph" added to try.

FEBRUARY 29

I have made many promises to reach out to the troubled, the sick and the hungry, Lord. Now steer me onto the path of action. Amen

The difference between smart people and dumb people isn't that smart people don't make mistakes. They just don't keep making the same mistakes over and over again.

NOVEMBER 2

O Father, grant me the gift of compassion and understanding. You understand and forgive so much, please guide me now. Amen

If you can't convince them
— confuse them.
Harry S. Truman

MARCH 1

Dear Father, Help me to focus on the happy things of life; not just in the early morning but all through the day. Amen

Experience is what you get when you didn't get what you wanted.

NOVEMBER 1

Dear Lord, my children are growing and feel ready to spread their wings. Grant me the courage to let them fly and I pray they will follow You. Amen

Before you have an argument with your boss, take a good look at both sides — his side and the outside.

MARCH 2

As I pray for my loved ones, O Lord, I visualize them as happy, secure and fulfilled. I commit them to Your care and know Your infinite love is with them. Amen

One is tolerant only of that which does not concern him.

OCTOBER 31

Heavenly Father, I know You are ever near and close to my heart. I need Thee, I cherish Thee. Amen

Rule of failure: If at first you don't succeed, destroy all evidence that you tried.

MARCH 3

When my world is at its darkest, Father, I need Thy loving hand on my shoulder and Thy blessed assurance that "this too shall pass". Amen

The man who knows "how" will always have a job. The man who knows "why" will always be his boss.

OCTOBER 30

Dear Father, cleanse my mind of anxieties and broodings. Help me to forgive myself for my transgressions and give me the courage to ask those whom I have offended for forgiveness. Amen

America is a land of opportunity,
if you're a business
man in Japan.

MARCH 4

Dear Lord, I pray that You will let me live a full and productive life on earth; and I thank You for the assurance of a life with Thee. Amen

If at first you don't succeed — find someone who knows what he's doing.

OCTOBER 29

Lord, like everyone else I have meaningless relationships and unnecessary self-imposed obligations. Help me to sort them out. Give me the courage to discard that which is useless and embrace that which is meaningful and satisfying. Amen

Is there anything more embarrassing than watching your boss do something you said couldn't be done?

MARCH 5

I pray that today I will make a difference in just one person's life; that I will have lessened their burdens and made their day happier. Amen

The only thing wrong with doing nothing is that you never know when you're finished.

OCTOBER 28

Father in Heaven, teach me not to pray for more but rather to be thankful for all You have bestowed upon me. Amen

The mark of a true M.B.A. is that he is often wrong but seldom in doubt.

MARCH 6

Lord, the best gift from You to all of us are the people who love us. Thank You for such a wonderful gift. Amen

Those who think they know it all are
very annoying to those who do.

OCTOBER 27

Lord, I need a push to help someone who is lonely or sad. Instill in me the right words and the compassion that will ease pain. Amen

There is no job so simple that it cannot be done wrong.

MARCH 7

Father, I need Your guidance through this day. Thy wisdom is much greater than mine. Amen

The way some people find fault, you'd think there was a reward.

OCTOBER 26

Gracious Lord, You have taught us that kind words reveal our thoughts and reflect what is in our heart and soul. Let me send kind words on their way today to better someone's life. Amen

Law of Destiny: Glory may be fleeting, but obscurity is forever.

MARCH 8

Sometimes I feel overwhelmed by the challenges facing me, O Lord. It is then that I especially need Your guidance. Amen

It's not whether you win or lose, but how you place the blame.

OCTOBER 25

Eternal Spirit, in my solitude I hear Your gentle voice, see Your kindly smile and feel Your comforting hand on my shoulder. I know You are with me always. Amen

The closest to perfection a person ever comes is when he fills out a job application form.

MARCH 9

Father guide me to live a practical life as You have taught us. Help me to erase the unkind thoughts that often enter my heart. Amen

Years make us old, people make us wise.

OCTOBER 24

O God, You know my strengths my weaknesses and my secret thoughts, and my selfish desire — yet You love me. Thank You. Amen

Blessed are the young, for they shall inherit the national debt.

MARCH 10

I shall try to remember, Dear Lord, that You do not send trouble my way, but rather the strength to bear it. Amen

Nothing is opened more often by mistake than the mouth.

OCTOBER 23

Father in heaven, open my eyes so I may see the beauty surrounding me, open my ears so I may hear all the joyous sounds of Your world. Slow me down so that I have time to revel in Your glorious world. Amen

The first screw to get loose in your head is the one that holds your tongue in place.

MARCH 11

Give me strength, Dear Lord to be a true Christian when it is easier to be otherwise. Amen

Save your money — someday it may be worth something.

OCTOBER 22

Friendship is to be treasured. Today, Dear Lord, I give thanks for all the friends in my life. Please protect them from harm. Amen

A good business manager hires
optimists as salespeople
and pessimists to run
the credit department.

MARCH 12

Dear God, help me to forget my painful memories. Let me bear in mind there is no joy in re-living unpleasant times. Amen

Success is just a matter of luck — just ask any failure.

OCTOBER 21

Dear Father, help me to always be aware of the marvels of my life now and not when I am in the depths of despair. Amen

If people listened to themselves more often, they would talk less.

MARCH 13

Walk beside me today, Lord, and show me the way to contentment and serenity. Amen

No job is too small to botch.

OCTOBER 20

I thank You Lord for giving me so many people and so many opportunities to love. Grant that I do not fail them. Amen

True wealth is not so much having talent, ambition and a bit of luck, as it is having lots of money.

MARCH 14

Father, help me to bury all bitter and unkind thoughts. Guide me all this day and keep me free from self-pity. Amen

There is always an easy solution to
every problem —
neat, plausible or wrong.

OCTOBER 19

When I am afraid, Lord, it means I have strayed away from You. Please help me to stay near You and grant me the faith that You will protect me. Amen

Always look for the calculations that go with the calculated risks.

MARCH 15

Dear Lord, You are here — ever near, close to my heart. I cherish Thee and need Thee. Thank You for Your care. Amen

The ignorant always seem so certain
and the intelligent so uncertain.

OCTOBER 18

Gracious Lord, You have given me hope and Your love for me has made me whole. Thank You for holding me up. Amen

Nobody ever puts out a sign that
says "NICE DOG".

MARCH 16

Lord, I know that ultimately time is all we have — help me to savor it not save it. Amen

The best investment opportunities are encountered when you are broke.

OCTOBER 17

Dear Father, when I center my life on You, my days are flooded with vitality. Thank You for Your tender mercies. Amen

If you want to avoid suspicion, do not stoop to tie your shoe in a melon patch.

MARCH 17

Father, I know I am too quick to see the faults in others. Help me to see my own faults just as clearly and instill in me the desire to shed my faults. Amen

Do it tomorrow — you've made enough mistakes for today.

OCTOBER 16

Precious Lord, don't let me take this wonderful life for granted. I pause now to say a prayer of thanks. Amen

Anger is never without reason, but seldom with a good one.

MARCH 18

I need to remember Dear Lord, that You are always within calling distance and are ready to listen whenever I ask. Amen

There are no absolute answers to
life — just revelations.

OCTOBER 15

Lord, make me eager to hear Your voice and follow Your holy words in my daily life. One distraction after another fills my thoughts. Grant me grace to hear Your loving voice within my soul. Amen

A hole in the bottom of a bird's nest usually means she enjoys laying eggs, but is not very fond of children.

MARCH 19

Father, I need to remember that You replenish love in me as I give love to others. Teach me to serve You joyfully. Amen

The light at the end of the tunnel could turn out to be the headlight of an oncoming train.

OCTOBER 14

Father, I joyfully put my complete trust in You. You have a purpose for my life — open my heart and my eyes to that purpose. Amen

If we had our life to live over,
we'd probably make the
same mistakes sooner.

MARCH 20

Dear Lord, I feel burdened by my sins and pray for Your merciful forgiveness. Help me to forgive myself and walk with You. Amen

There is always free cheese
in a mousetrap.

OCTOBER 13

Lord, when my dreams are shattered, walk beside me, comfort me and show me the way to other dreams and fulfillment. Amen

It's not possible to make anything foolproof, because fools are so ingenious.

MARCH 21

Father, I need to remember that I can trust Your judgment every day. If things I pray for are not granted, help me to accept that it is because You in Your wisdom have deemed it so. Amen

Family units are like banks. If you take out more than you put in they go broke.

OCTOBER 12

Father, I know I am too quick to see the faults in others. Help me to see my own faults just as clearly and instill in me the desire to correct my faults. Amen

A road map tells you everything except how to refold it.

MARCH 22

Lord, make me eager to hear Your voice and follow Your holy words in my daily life. One distraction after another fills my thoughts. Open my heart and enter in. Amen

A sure formula for success — think of a product that costs a dime, sells for a dollar and is habit forming.

OCTOBER 11

Heavenly Father, help me to remember to set aside time for You today. Silence my busy mind, calm me and let me feel Your loving presence. Amen

A bird in the hand is safer
than one overhead.

MARCH 23

Dear Lord, help me to trust You so that I may feel You are with me always and therefore I need not fear. Amen

A martyr is a person married to a saint.

OCTOBER 10

Dear Lord, are my troubles really opportunities in disguise? Help me to see beyond these painful times and to trust in Your guidance. Amen

God made man at the end of the week,
when he was tired.

MARCH 24

O Lord, mold me while I am silent, listening and calm, to be the person You planned for me to be. Amen

Sometimes we all feel like a
snapdragon — no snap
and everything draggin'.

OCTOBER 9

Heavenly Father, there are times when I want to share experiences and thoughts with other people but often I do not feel they will understand. I am thankful I can talk with You and feel Your understanding. Amen

If someone says: "I'm expensive"
— believe them.

MARCH 25

Dear Father, help me to be quiet long enough and with enough openness to hear You in my heart. Amen

Young priests listening to confessions
must learn to refrain
from saying "Wow!"

OCTOBER 8

I need to remember that God is always within calling distance and that He is ready to listen whenever I call His name. Amen

Never put off till tomorrow that you can avoid altogether.

MARCH 26

Loving Father make me sensitive to the cries for help around me. Reinforce my desire and will to respond. Amen

God gives every bird his food, but He doesn't throw it into the nest.

OCTOBER 7

O Father, open my eyes to the needs of others and let me respond with an open heart. Amen

The main cause of problems is solutions.

MARCH 27

Dear Lord, my strength and my redeemer,
help me to live so that I will always feel
Your goodness and might. Amen

There are two periods when fishing is
good: before you get there and
after you leave.

OCTOBER 6

Dear Lord, quiet my mind in this time of meditation with You. Let Your Spirit communicate with my Spirit — help me grow in Your way. Amen

An idea is a curious thing — it will not work unless you do.

MARCH 28

Holy Father, I pray that Thy will be done here on earth; now show me how to do my part. Amen

An executive is that type of person
who solves more problems
than he creates.

OCTOBER 5

Merciful Father, I thank You for the path out of the darkness. It is only when I feel Your love that my path is full of light. Amen

There is a difference between an open mind and a hole in the head.

MARCH 29

Precious Lord, I need to remember that I was not put on earth to make everyone happy, but rather to please You with kindness and compassion toward those who need it most. Amen

Why in the world is it always the third car back that is the first to see the light turn green?

OCTOBER 4

Lord, teach me to be content with the work I accomplish today. Let me not begrudge interruptions but rather welcome them as a time of communion with those around me. Amen

Common sense is the least common of all senses.

MARCH 30

Dear Father, help me to resist temptations that I know are morally wrong. Strengthen me with Thy powerful hand. Amen

There are seven ways to warm your feet in February. Dipping them in the Caribbean is one. If you can afford that, forget the other six.

OCTOBER 3

Dear Father, teach me to be a loving, caring compassionate follower of Your teachings — not in words but in deeds. Amen

Toys are so sophisticated these days that they can play with each other.

MARCH 31

O Lord, when my words and deeds contradict each other, make me aware of Your displeasure. Amen

Two can live as cheaply as one, but only half as long.

OCTOBER 2

Father, when I feel alone and burdened let me feel your gentle touch. Be with me this day as I make decisions that involve those who trust me. Amen

Mondays are the potholes in the road of life.

APRIL 1

Dear Lord, I pray for courage to stop destructive gossip. Should I hear unfounded gossip, let me object firmly but without being self-righteous. Amen

Now about that adage — "If you have to ask, you can't afford it" — whoever expected it to apply to a postage stamp?

OCTOBER 1

Dear Lord, I need to remember that love is replenished in me as I give love to others. Teach me to serve You joyfully. Amen

If you're stopped by the police, shut off your engine and put your mouth in neutral.

APRIL 2

O Lord, help me to stop thinking that everything depends on me. I often forget that everyone is just as capable as I and that the world will one day go on without me. Amen

One good thing about talking to yourself is that you always have a rapt audience.

SEPTEMBER 30

Dear Lord, my moments of true peace are those spent with You. You ease the pain in my tormented heart. I pray for those who have hurt me and I pray that I will be forgiving. Amen

Before you borrow money from a friend, decide which you need more.

APRIL 3

Dear Father, I regret the hateful words I have spoken. Help me to silence my acid tongue and offer sincere apologies to those I have hurt — even in a small way. Amen

The smartest advice on raising children is to enjoy them while they are still on your side.

SEPTEMBER 29

Father, I know that peace comes with forgiveness. Open my heart to accept the imperfections in others just as You accept my imperfections. Amen

Never eat any product on which the listed ingredients cover more than one-third of the package.

APRIL 4

Dear Lord, when I am hurting and confused, may I have the courage to share that hurt with my loved ones. Help me to remember they are not mind readers and that they may not be able to solve my problems, but can be supportive. Amen

Talk is cheap because the supply exceeds the demand.

SEPTEMBER 28

I give thanks to Thee, Dear Lord, for Thy healing embrace. Today I will place all my worries at Your feet. Amen

A person who is always up in the air
and harping on something is not
necessarily an angel.

APRIL 5

O Father in Heaven, when the way is dark and confusing, lead me into Your light and guide me out of the darkness. Amen

We all have the strength to endure the misfortunes of others.

SEPTEMBER 27

Father in heaven, You have given me so many material things, now I pray for those things that will help me grow — understanding, kindness and love. Amen

People do not usually reject the Bible because it contradicts itself, but because it contradicts them.

APRIL 6

O Lord, when I fail in my efforts, let me not feel that You have abandoned me. I just ask for the courage to try again. Amen

The brain is a wonderful organ; it starts working the moment you get up in the morning and does not stop until you get to work.

SEPTEMBER 26

Lord, I am hurting. I know I cannot change the situation, but how can I bear the hurt? Please walk beside me and help me find peace. Amen

Every person should have a special cemetery plot in which to bury the faults of friends and loved ones.

APRIL 7

Lord, sometimes I fail to love someone who really needs love. Forgive me when I fail to love. But I ask also, that You help me to find the love I need. Amen

Old people shouldn't eat health foods;
they need all the preservatives
they can get.

SEPTEMBER 25

O God, there are times when You seem so far away. I want to feel your nearness. Take my hand and bring me closer to You. I need to feel Your warmth. Amen

Nowadays the only time people seem to get on their knees is when looking for a contact lens.

APRIL 8

Father, help me to distinguish between what is important and the glitter. It is so easy to forget and the temptations for the glitter seem to be always there. Amen

What this country needs is a few unemployed politicians.

SEPTEMBER 24

O Lord, please do not let any day pass without my showing kindness to someone — a kindness that was not asked for and unexpected. Amen

If God believed in permissiveness,
he would have given us
the Ten Suggestions.

APRIL 9

Help me to trust you Dear Lord, so that I may know You are always with me and I need not fear. Amen

If the meek inherit the earth, how long will they stay meek after they get it?

SEPTEMBER 23

Father, today help me to remember to tell someone they are appreciated and that I am grateful for their friendship and service. Amen

Children should be heard, not obscene.

APRIL 10

Dear Father, help me to be a true friend to someone today — someone who is troubled, lonely or frightened. Amen

And that's the world in a nutshell —
an appropriate receptacle.

SEPTEMBER 22

Dear Lord, I come to You when I'm troubled and then forget You when life is bright. I will try to be thankful every day. Thank You for never forgetting me. Amen

Don't ever stand up to be counted or someone will take your seat.

APRIL 11

O God, I thank You for Your love, patience and forgiveness. Now help me to be loving, patient and forgiving with others. Amen

America has been discovered before,
but it's always been hushed up.

Oscar Wilde

SEPTEMBER 21

Dear Lord, I know that without You beside me I could not face the day before me unafraid. Thank You for courage and Thy blessed guidance. Amen

What we learn after we know it all,
is what counts.

APRIL 12

Heavenly Father, help me to embrace the
qualities that will make my life a happier
one — love, kindness, caring, integrity,
honesty, and trust. Amen

Nobody has ever bet enough on
a winning horse.

SEPTEMBER 20

Father, help me to bury and forget all bitter and unkind thoughts. Stay by my side and guide me all this day. Amen

Old people know more about being
young than young people know
about being old.

APRIL 13

Heavenly Father, teach me to love people regardless of their social rank. Instill in me the desire to help those who have so very little.

It is better to be a coward for a minute
than dead for the rest of your life.
An Irish Proverb

SEPTEMBER 19

Dear Lord, my troubles are real. How can I keep from being overwhelmed by them? Let me feel your comforting embrace and let me feel that you are lightening my burden. Amen

If it smells bad and is sticky, it will eventually find its way onto your shoes or your child's shoes.

APRIL 14

Dear Father, I search for Your purpose for me. Help me to see and accept that purpose and the will to pursue it. Amen

The reason grandparents and grandchildren get along so well is that they have a common enemy.

SEPTEMBER 18

Dear Father, I often feel frustrated when my efforts don't bring the results I try to achieve. Help me to hang in there with patience and perseverance. Amen

Education is the process of
moving from cocksure
to thoughtful uncertainty.

APRIL 15

Father in Heaven, there are times when I act on the urge to put others "in their place". Help me to put myself in their place instead. Amen

There's nothing wrong with teenagers that reasoning with them won't aggravate.

SEPTEMBER 17

Lord, You have given me so much, but I have not given to those who have so much less. Loosen my grasping hand so that I may know the joy of giving. Amen

Any law enacted with more than fifty words contains at least one loophole.

APRIL 16

There are times Dear Lord, when I am in doubt. Give me the assurance again that Your Spirit will always be with me to guide, strengthen, forgive and love me. Amen

You can buy flattery but envy
must be earned.

SEPTEMBER 16

O Lord, sometimes I grow weary of doing good things and not receiving thanks in return. And yet, I receive so much more than I give. I am the one who should give thanks. Amen

A hug is a perfect gift — one size fits all and nobody minds if you give it back.

APRIL 17

Dear Lord, I do not always feel the love of others but I am very grateful to You for Your surrounding love. Amen

He was a perfect pessimist —
a real no-it-all.

SEPTEMBER 15

Dear Lord, grant me the wisdom to set realistic goals and the determination and patience to work toward those goals. Amen

A man who thinks he is smarter than
his wife has a very smart wife.

APRIL 18

Dear Father, help me to remember that You ask us to be available, not perfect. Urge me on as I extend an uplifting hand to someone today who needs it. Amen

Doing business without advertising is
like winking at a girl in the dark —
you know what you are doing, but
nobody else does.

SEPTEMBER 14

Heavenly Father, when I need peace and comforting, take my hand and let me feel Your loving touch. Days are the most fulfilling when I feel You beside me. Amen

You know you are getting old when the candles cost more than the cake.

APRIL 19

O Father, help me to respond in love to the needs of others. May my caring refresh someone's life today. Amen

You have to know what's biting you before you reach for a remedy.

SEPTEMBER 13

Walk with me, talk with me, Dear Lord, and teach me how to be merciful. Let me not condemn but rather understand those who have hurt me. Amen.

They say there are lots of good fish in the sea — but who wants to go out with fish?

APRIL 20

O Lord, I am ever grateful to you for being my friend, companion and guide. Thank You for thinking I am worthy of Your deep love. Amen

Even if you're on the right track, you'll get run over if you just sit there.

SEPTEMBER 12

Father in heaven, forgive me for unkind remarks I say about others. Help me to see the goodness in those with whom I disagree. Amen

A wallet is a device that permits you to lose all your valuables at the same time.

APRIL 21

Dear Father, I have not always lived up to my commitment and yet the times when I feel scared, unsure, frustrated or depressed, You are beside me. Amen

Experience is the name everyone gives
to their mistakes.

SEPTEMBER 11

Dear Lord, whatever good I do today is my gift to You and to myself. Help me to remember that true happiness comes when we give of ourselves. Amen

The simplest toy that even the youngest child can operate is called a grandparent.

APRIL 22

Thank You for the gift of health and life,
Dear Lord, and for the strength to do my
work and Yours. Amen

Expecting success without hard work
is like trying to harvest where
you haven't planted.

SEPTEMBER 10

Heavenly Father, I spend far too much time worrying. Help me to develop a more positive outlook with trust and hope. Amen

The secret of happiness is being content with what you get —
so get plenty.

APRIL 23

Dear Lord, You are my hope, my trust, my strength, my comfort and my most faithful helper in every need. Amen

If it goes without saying, let it.

SEPTEMBER 9

Precious Lord, help me to rise above those who are thoughtless and hurtful. Teach me how to forgive them as You forgive me. Amen

Success covers a multitude of blunders.

APRIL 24

Dear Father, let laughter fill my home, for laughter is the heartbeat of a home and the fuel for the warmth there. Amen

Committee work is like a soft chair — easy to get into but hard to get out of.

SEPTEMBER 8

I know You answer my prayers, Lord. Help me to accept Your answers with trust, especially when the answer is "no". Amen

You may feel as though you are adrift
but be thankful you are still afloat.

APRIL 25

Heavenly Father, stay close to those who are grieving and release them from their sorrow. Heartache is draining and makes life lonelier. Hear my prayer. Amen

You know the tax loopholes are too large when you see people driving their fortunes through them.

SEPTEMBER 7

Father in heaven, I thank You for Your outstretched hand. Your love enfolds me and fills my heart with peace. Amen

A friend is someone who doesn't buy your child a drum for Christmas.

APRIL 26

O Lord, don't let me be too busy to love —
show me how to encourage those who are
discouraged and cry out to You. Amen

On your way up the ladder of success
watch out for the person behind you.

SEPTEMBER 6

Dear Father, forgive me for the sin of indifference and put me to work to help those less fortunate than I. Amen

An optimist is the guy who can always
see the bright side of
other people's problems.

APRIL 27

O Lord, make me a nice person for the right reasons; not to be popular or to be loved or liked, but because being a nice person feels so good. Amen

If you want to keep a friend, never suggest what's wrong with her children.

SEPTEMBER 5

Dear Lord, when bad things happen to me, help me to understand that You are not punishing me. I have faith that You will give me the strength to endure all things. Amen

We all have undeveloped territory —
it's under our hat.

APRIL 28

Father, help me not to put too much importance in possessions. Let me never forget that possessions are meant to enhance life, not be the focal part of living. Amen

Some men are so handy around the house they are able to fix the same thing over and over again.

SEPTEMBER 4

O Father, I need to be reminded that I am important and loved by You; and that You are with me always. Amen

A loving husband is one who remembers his wife's birthday, but forgets which one.

APRIL 29

Thank You Lord, for giving me so many people to love. I pray I will not fail them when they are in need of help. Amen

This is not to defend the devil, but in all fairness it must be said that all the books about the devil were written by God's friends.

SEPTEMBER 3

Dear Lord, I pray for Your help in learning patience. It is not easy for me and I cannot improve without Your help. Amen

What this country needs is a set of brakes that will stop the car behind us.

APRIL 30

Lord, keep me from being a grim and cheerless person, unable to see the funny side, even when things go wrong. Help me to see the comedy of my errors. Amen

Treat your family like friends and your friends like family.

SEPTEMBER 2

Heavenly Father, help me to remember that You are in control. Only when I surrender my life to You will I truly start living. Amen

Telling a teen-ager the facts of life is like giving a fish a bath.

MAY 1

Father, when I have been unjustly accused or scolded, I feel so humiliated and unworthy. Help me to restore my self-esteem. Amen

After forty, life is just a
physical maintenance job.

SEPTEMBER 1

Merciful Father, harboring regrets and grudges does not benefit me. Help me to let go of unhappy thoughts that are so destructive. Amen

Santa Claus comes to us
under many names:
Kris Kringle, St. Nicholas, MasterCard.

MAY 2

Dear Lord, help me to be more understanding of my loved ones' limitations. Keep me from asking more of them than they are equipped to give. Amen

Most of us don't mind getting older;
but we do mind having aging children.

AUGUST 31

Precious Lord, help me to care for and love those I find unlovable, for they need it most of all. Amen

From the time an infant tries to get his toes in his mouth, life is a continual struggle to make both ends meet.

MAY 3

Lord, sometimes I have compared my lot with others. Help me to remember that every life has its drawbacks and burdens. I know that no one has everything and never will I. Amen

In this world it rains on the Just and
the Unjust alike,
but the Unjust have
the Justs' umbrellas.

AUGUST 30

Dear Lord, I often envy others for their possessions. I know this is wrong. Forgive me and teach me not to covet. Amen

Nothing is as difficult to do gracefully
as getting off your high horse.

MAY 4

I pray for the hungry, Dear Lord. I ask that you press me into helpful action such as being a supplier to the food shelves. Amen

Fresh flowers are acceptable. Fresh mouths are not.

AUGUST 29

Dear Lord, instill in me the trust I am so fearful of extending to You. It isn't always easy to remember that You care. Amen

Handle them carefully, for words have more power than atom bombs.

MAY 5

Deliver me from gossiping, Lord, and give me the moral strength to defend the person being gossiped about. Amen

Mother-daughter dresses are cute —
for about 10 minutes.

AUGUST 28

Every day I accept Your gifts, Lord, and take Your generosity for granted. Now help me to see the needs of others and to serve them as You serve me. Amen

Ask God's blessings on your work,
but don't ask Him to
do it for you.

MAY 6

O Lord, if I hurt today please be my refuge, my strength and my consolation. I put my trust in Thee. Amen

All children are born with a hearing problem. They can hear everyone's mother but their own.

AUGUST 27

Be with me Lord, in my difficult decisions.
I have fears of having to live with wrong
choices. Be my guide and help me. Amen

Laughter is a tranquilizer with
no side effects.

MAY 7

Father, a friend is deeply troubled and although I've listened to her problems many times, soften my heart and grant me patience to listen again if she needs me. Amen

You may outgrow your parents' laps,
but you'll never outgrow their hearts.

AUGUST 26

Heavenly Father, may I always be aware of Your presence. I need Your love and support every day. Amen

The most important things in the world, aren't things.

MAY 8

Dear Lord, You've put so much beauty into our world, let me take time to see it and share it. Today I will bring a flower to a friend who needs cheering. Amen

There's nothing sweeter than the patter
of little feet...going home.

AUGUST 25

Eternal God, I feel insecure and afraid of sharing my worldly goods. Help me find the confidence that You will always provide and that sharing is Your way. Amen

The price of sin is everlasting damnation, but that's one price that never goes up.

MAY 9

Our Father, I need to feel the joy of Your presence — Your gentle voice of assurance and the comfort of Your arms enfolding me. Be with me today. Amen

If you've been together long enough to be on your second bottle of Tabasco sauce, you can bet your marriage will last.

AUGUST 24

Dear Father, every day I have opportunities to show my appreciation for someone. I pray that I will not ignore any of these opportunities. All I ask in return is a sense of blessing. Amen

Nothing in the world can replace the
modern swimsuit, and
it practically has.

MAY 10

Merciful Lord, fill my heart with peace and as I go about my day let me be tolerant toward all those I meet. Amen

The second wife always has
a cleaning lady.

AUGUST 23

Heavenly Father, I need to let go of my grievances. How empty are my days when I spend time nursing hurts. How much better I feel when I pocket my pride and forgive. Amen

One of the advantages of a clean life is that you can distinguish between flu and a hangover.

MAY 11

Dear Father, I know I have not done the things you would have me do and I have done those things which did not please You. For this I pray for forgiveness. Amen

When you have an argument with your spouse, don't drag things out of your mental museum.

AUGUST 22

Dear Lord, bless this day that I am about to begin. Bless my family and keep them from harm. Bless my friends and co-workers. Guide us all day to do the things that please you. Amen

The longest wait in the world is when the nurse tells you to take off your clothes because the doctor will be with you in a moment.

MAY 12

Lord, I feel Your love within me and it fills me with strength and tranquility. Thank You for your supporting embrace. Amen

Most love triangles are wrecktangles.

AUGUST 21

Heavenly Spirit, open my eyes, my ears and heart to those who are troubled. Show me how to make their life better, according to Your teachings. Amen

The quickest way to learn speed reading is to get an unexpected letter from the IRS.

MAY 13

Help me Father, to feel that You have forgiven me for all my mistakes and help me to forgive myself. I pray for a life of peace and joy. Amen

Counterfeit money can always be called homemade bread.

AUGUST 20

Gracious Lord, help me to gather all my worries into the daylight hours and turn them over to You before I go to bed. Amen

About the only thing that can halt an outrageous fad among the young is for adults to adopt it.

MAY 14

I want to be Your follower, Heavenly Father. Take my hand and tune me in to the needs of the suffering and hungry. When I serve them, I serve You also. Amen

August is that time of year when you
go to turn on the air conditioner
and it already is.

AUGUST 19

Dear Father, when I lose my way I pray that You will strengthen my wavering spirit and heighten my understanding so that I may ever be Your loving child. Amen

Ever notice how quickly kids learn to
drive a car, yet cannot understand
the lawn mower, snow blower
or vacuum cleaner?

MAY 15

Heavenly Father, thank You for Your healing love. I look to You for comfort and hope and You never fail me. Amen

With jeans there's no problem finding
the right pair — one size hurts all.

AUGUST 18

Dear Lord, help me to remember that though we may have our differences we are all Your children and that we must love one another as You love us. Amen

Why is it that the people who have an hour to waste usually try to spend it with someone who does not?

MAY 16

Dear Father, You have quieted my fears and helped me achieve peace in my heart. Thank You for Your care. Amen

Ever wonder if taxation without
representation might
have been cheaper?

AUGUST 17

O Father In Heaven, I try to remember that You expect more of me than just a fleeting prayer. Thank You for Your many blessings and instill in me a grateful heart. Amen

Ever notice that nothing makes a boss
more admired than his
being within earshot?

MAY 17

Lord, when my hopes have been dashed to pieces and my dreams shattered keep me close to you and let me feel the flow of Your strength into my heart. Amen

Now take the word "indolence". It makes laziness seem classy.

AUGUST 16

Father, You know what I say, what I do and what I think and feel. I pray that the way I live pleases You. Amen

It's called "PANDORA'S RULE": Never open a box you didn't close.

MAY 18

Father, help me to remember that everyone faces trials and tribulations — not only I. I know You will give me the courage to live one day at a time. Amen

Victory goes to the player who makes the next-to-last mistake.

AUGUST 15

Dear Lord, I will try to look forward to the changes in my life without fear . . . I know You will lead me safely up every path. Amen

If we could sell our experiences for
what they cost us, we'd
all be millionaires.

MAY 19

Father In Heaven, let me set aside my wants for just this one day and with genuine effort and caring, make it a better day for someone else. Amen

You know you have had too much rain when the ducks are riding in boats.

AUGUST 14

O Lord, may loving be my reason for living. I ask that You warm my heart, soften my rigid walls and bend my pride. Amen

Skillful listening is the best remedy for loneliness, loquaciousness and laryngitis.

MAY 20

Dear Lord, help me to build bridges, not walls and guide me across those bridges to help someone in need. Amen

Never go to bed mad.
Stay up and fight.

AUGUST 13

Dear Lord, my heart clings to You. I know
You are with me always and when You touch
my soul, I am strengthened. Amen

Happiness is never stopping to
think if you are.

MAY 21

Dear Lord, You have shown me that there is no greater deed than the one done for others. With Your help, may I always be willing to give of myself as You give to me. Amen

The two hardest things to handle in life
are failure and success.

AUGUST 12

*O Lord, when I am surrounded by shadows,
help me to trust and not be afraid. Amen*

Injustice is relatively easy to bear; what
stings is justice.

MAY 22

O Father, I pray that You will help me not to be so self-centered. Fill me with the desire to think of others and to help them however I am able. Amen

There is no pleasure in having nothing to do; the fun is having lots to do and not doing it.

AUGUST 11

Lord, I know that You are everywhere and if I cry out that I cannot find You it is because I have not completely opened my heart to You. Amen

Man never made any material as resilient as the human spirit.

MAY 23

Dear Lord, I am often blind to Your presence in my life and to the daily joys with which You bless me. Amen

Husbands and wives are like fires.
They go out if unattended.

AUGUST 10

Dear Lord, help me make a difference in someone's life so that they will be glad I am their friend. Amen

Sometimes you have to be silent in order to be heard.

MAY 24

I pray that I will always be worthy of Your precious love. Keep me ever faithful, O Lord, and help me to always try to give You my best. Amen.

As you slide down the banister of life,
don't get a splinter in your career.

AUGUST 9

Dear Lord, help me to see past the surface and into the beauty of human hearts as You do. Amen

Tact is the art of making guests feel at home when that's where you wish they were.

MAY 25

Father, keeping the promises I have made to You is my responsibility not Yours. Instill in me the determination to keep those promises. Amen

The tongue — we spend three years learning how to use it and the rest of our lives learning how to control it.

AUGUST 8

Lord, I ask for Your Mercy. Wash away my sins so that they vanish completely from my soul and my mind. Amen

Prayer is when you talk to God;
meditation is when you listen to God.

MAY 26

Dear Father, I truly mean to keep all the promises I have made to You. Put me to work fulfilling those promises. Amen

What's to be done? Everyone wants to go to heaven, but nobody wants to die.

AUGUST 7

Thank You Lord, for giving me so many people to love. I pray that I will not fail them. Amen

Frustration is when the same snow that covers the ski slopes makes the road to them impassable.

MAY 27

When my burden seems too heavy to carry, you give me stamina to go on. You do not desert me when I call out to You. Amen

Management is the art of getting other people to do all the work.

AUGUST 6

Father, stay close to those who are grieving and release them from their sorrow. Heartache is draining and makes life lonelier. I pray You will help them. Amen

The test of your fairness is how fair you are to those who are not.

MAY 28

O Lord, when I am angry and upset, please calm me down. Help me to remember when I put my trust in You, You will see me through the day. Amen

There are some people in a fifty-fifty proposition, who insist on getting the hyphen too.

AUGUST 5

Dear Lord, help me not to put too much importance in possessions. Possessions are meant to enhance life, not be a focal part of living. Amen

There is no substitute for incomprehensible good luck.

MAY 29

Father in Heaven, help me to remember that the more faith I have, the more strength I have. Amen

A nickel goes a long way now. You can carry it around for days without finding a thing it will buy.

AUGUST 4

Let the laughter fill my home, Dear Lord,
for laughter is the heartbeat of a home and
the fuel for the warmth there. Amen

Education is learning what you didn't
even know you didn't know.

MAY 30

Merciful Lord, cleanse me from all the prejudices I harbor within me. Forgive me for all the injustices of my pride. Amen

Too bad the only people who know how to run the country are busy driving cabs or cutting hair.

AUGUST 3

Dear Lord, You are my hope, my trust, my strength, my comfort and my faithful helper in every need. Amen

Never trust too much in an overly modest man. A guy failing to toot his own horn may simply have a dead battery.

MAY 31

I live in the light of God. It guides me, directs me and shines through me. My mind and my heart are open to love and forgiveness. Amen

Nobody ever forgets where he buried the hatchet.

AUGUST 2

Father, don't let me be too busy to love.
Show me how to encourage those who are
discouraged and at the end of their rope.
Amen

The only way to live is to accept each
minute as an unrepeatable miracle,
which is exactly what it is — a
miracle and unrepeatable.

JUNE 1

Heavenly Father, do not forsake me as I start my day with overwhelming problems. Guide me with Your loving hands and protect me from harm. Amen

The best scientific theory is that the rings of Saturn are composed entirely of lost airline luggage.

AUGUST 1

Dear Lord, teach me that marvelous lesson that it is very possible I may be mistaken occasionally. Amen

Now and then it's good to pause in our pursuit of happiness and just be happy.

JUNE 2

Thank You, Dear Lord, for listening to me with love and patience. I pray for a thankful and grateful heart for Your blessings. Amen

Rivers in the United States are
so polluted that acid rain
makes them cleaner.

JULY 31

Keep me reasonably sweet, Dear Lord. I do not want to be a saint — some of them are so hard to live with — but a sour old person is very unappealing. Amen

One thought driven home is better than three left on base.

JUNE 3

Dear Lord, there are times when I hunger for faith, feel lost and lonely with doubt. Guide me through this darkness. Amen

Veni, Vida, Visa (we came, we saw, we went shopping)

JULY 30

Father, give me the ability to see good in unexpected places and talents in unexpected people. I ask for the grace to tell them so. Amen

Anyone all wrapped up in themselves,
is over dressed.

JUNE 4

If I get discouraged today, Lord, let me feel Thy presence and guidance. As I extend my hand, let me feel Your reassuring touch and abundant love. Amen

The trouble with speaking one's mind
is that it limits conversations.

JULY 29

Dear Lord, thank You for healing my hurt heart; for soothing my sorrow and for loving me. Amen

A happy marriage is the
world's best bargain.

JUNE 5

Loving Father, Your wisdom is mine to use if only I would take the time to read and listen to Your Word. Help me to live as the scriptures teach. Amen

Start a new diet — no more eating your own words, swallowing your pride or putting your foot in your mouth.

JULY 28

Father, I have an undesirable habit of thinking I must say something on every occasion. Help me to remember there is much to learn by listening. Amen

Laughter can be heard farther than weeping.

JUNE 6

Father, I pray that my words and actions will not hurt anyone today. If I cannot speak and act kindly, let me be silent. Amen

God wisely designed the human body
so that we can neither pat our own
backs nor kick ourselves too easily.

JULY 27

Father, release me from wanting to straighten out everybody's affairs. I need to remember I am not a judge. Amen

No sound concentrates so much spitefulness and malice into a very small volume as the panging of mosquitos.

JUNE 7

Dear Lord, sometimes I compare my life with that of another. Help me to appreciate my many blessings and remind me that I would not trade my life with any one else's if I could see behind their closed doors. Amen

Man is the only species who plants a crop he can't eat but still has to mow every week.

JULY 26

I pray for courage to speak up when I see or hear a wrong or an injustice. Let me not be silent Father, but rather try to right that wrong. Amen

Some people are the clinging-whine type.

JUNE 8

Heavenly Lord, I know I have a mission that You have bestowed upon just me. I pray that mission will be revealed to me so that I may do Your good works. Amen

Inside some of us is a thin person struggling to get out but he can usually be sedated with a few pieces of chocolate cake.

JULY 25

Lord, should I feel sorry for myself today, help me to remember that no one lives in perfection and that tomorrow is a new, untarnished day. Amen

Truce is better than friction.

JUNE 9

Dear Lord, teach me to trust You wherever I go; and wherever I go I shall do Your work. Amen

God doesn't have to put His name
on a sign in the corner of
a meadow because nobody
else makes meadows.

JULY 24

I rely on You, Dear Lord, and my work becomes pleasant. I rely on You, and my burdens fall away. Amen

You can be hurt only if you care a lot.

JUNE 10

Father, I know you have planned my purpose on earth — to be of service for my fellow-man. Now help me accept that responsibility and fulfill it. Amen

If you can't be kind, at least be vague.

JULY 23

Father, help me to be sensitive to the goodness in others and to be less critical of those whose priorities differ from mine. Amen

Some people are so persistent, they'd have the last word with an echo.

JUNE 11

Father In Heaven, do You want me to feed the hungry, find the lost, make music in the heart? Reveal your wishes in my heart so that I may do Your good works. Amen

The trouble with making mental notes
is that the ink fades so fast.

JULY 22

When I have hurt someone, Lord, help me to sincerely say "I'm sorry", and not sit in judgment and say the hurt was deserved. Amen

There are those whose train of thought
never leaves the depot.

JUNE 12

Dear Lord, I know You have not created me for nothing. Help me see Your purpose. Open my eyes and heart and guide me on to the path where I am most needed. Amen

Do you realize we can no longer teach
that what goes up must come down?

JULY 21

Lord, help me to understand that it is only by serving others in Your name that we find love, peace and joy in our faith and in our lives. Amen

The will of God will never lead you
where the grace of God
cannot keep you.

JUNE 13

O Father, I am a link in a chain that connects all of Your children. Lead me on the path to strengthen that connection. Amen

Most foreign countries, when they think of America, think of Dough-nations.

JULY 20

O Father, help me to be sensitive to the needs and pain of those around me. Guide me as I try to help them. Amen

Plan ahead — it wasn't raining when Noah built the ark.

JUNE 14

Lord, I need to remember that I am far from perfect, that I hurt and offend. Help me to be a better person. Amen

Why a man would want a wife is a mystery to some people. Why he would want two or more is a bigamystery.

JULY 19

Thank You Lord for Your gentle guidance.
With Your help I will accept worthy challenges.
Amen

Work rules:
1) The boss is always right.
2) If the boss is wrong,
see rule #1.

JUNE 15

Dear Father in Heaven, help me to be receptive to Your word — write it on my heart so that I may live my life to please You. Amen

How wise are Thy Commandments, O Lord. Each one of them applies to somebody I know.

JULY 18

Wash what is dirty. Water what is dry, Heal what is wounded. Soothe what is hurt. Dry tears that are shed. Warm what is cold. Guide what goes off the road. Love those who are least lovable because they need it most.

Did you know the 10 commandments
are not multiple choice?

JUNE 16

O Lord, help me to find You when I search for You. I come to You searching for courage and comfort to carry me through this day. Amen

The entire sum of existence is the magic of being needed by just one person.

JULY 17

O Father, thank You for being near me when I reach out to you for comfort. When I fall apart you miraculously put me back together again. Amen

People don't plan to fail — they simply fail to plan.

JUNE 17

I will take time today to reach out to someone who is ill, who is frightened or who is lonely. Amen

No noise is so emphatic as one you are trying not to listen to.

JULY 16

Dear Father, help me to remember that You are at work within me and around me each day, even when I am blind to Thy good. Amen

If you have a rose to give, give it today
for tomorrow may be too late.

JUNE 18

Holy Father, I ask for courage to let you control my life. If I have lost faith in You, even for a moment, restore it. Amen

On the edge of a precipice, only a fool does cartwheels.

JULY 15

Father I need to be reminded that You are not my servant, but rather that I am Your servant, and to serve Your children is to please You. Amen

Optimism: A cheerful frame of mind that enables a tea kettle to sing even though it's in hot water up to its nose.

JUNE 19

Dear Father, instill in me that I can depend on you always; that you will share my joys and my sorrows. Amen

Anticipating is even more
fun than recollecting.

JULY 14

Dear Lord, help me in my distress, open my heart so that I may feel Your caring, loving Spirit. Amen

People who brag about their ancestors are like carrots — the best part of them is underground.

JUNE 20

Dear Lord, those of Your children who are hungry — let me feed them. Those who are hurt, let me comfort them. Amen

The difference between dogs and cats
is that dogs come when they're called.
Cats take a message and
get back to you.

JULY 13

Father, help me to stop worrying about money. Instill in me the faith and confidence that You always provide. Amen

Lord, give me strength to resist
temptation, but not just yet.

JUNE 21

Father, I am often envious of those who seem to have so much more than I. Teach me to count my blessings and share with those who have so much less than I. Amen

Part of the happiness of life consists
not in fighting battles but in avoiding
them. A masterly retreat
is in itself a victory.

JULY 12

You have opened my heart, Dear Lord; now enter there and grant me peace. Amen

Whenever you can,
hang around the lucky.
A Chinese proverb

JUNE 22

Lord, I often recall old hurts. Help me to remember that nothing is gained by living in the past. Teach me how to truly forgive and forget. Amen

Think no evil, see no evil, hear no evil — and you will never write a best-selling novel.

JULY 11

O God, sometimes doubt seems to consume me. Help me not to make faith dependent upon the things I pray for and don't get. Amen

What this country needs is a course
on defending yourself from folks
who've had assertive training.

JUNE 23

O Lord, wherever I travel in life, whenever I feel lonely or distressed, help me to remember that You are always with me. Amen

Some people look for divine guidance in the Ten Commandments, but most are looking for loopholes.

JULY 10

Dear Lord, help me to see the good in those whose lives touch mine. Banish criticism from my heart and mind. Amen

Most of us believe everyone should
work — especially those
who have jobs.

JUNE 24

Dear Lord, I ask forgiveness for not doing many things that I should have done and for doing many things I did but should not have done. I'm truly ashamed. Amen

Gather ye rosebuds where ye may;
florists are very expensive.

JULY 9

Father in heaven, thank You for lightening my burdens. Thank You for hearing me when I cry out to You in pain. Thank You for loving me. Amen

Your problems only defeat you when
you let them lean on you.

JUNE 25

O God, I pray for the courage to embrace dreams, the strength to sacrifice for them and the determination to fulfill them. Amen

Absence makes the heart go wander.

JULY 8

Dear Father, when I am wrong make me willing to admit it and when I am right, make me easy to live with. Amen

You are getting old when you talk to yourself and you listen.

JUNE 26

Holy Lord, often I do not hear the silent cries for help of those around me. Quiet me and make me more aware of those who are hurting. Amen

People who talk like walking encyclopedias should remember that reference books rarely circulate.

JULY 7

O Lord, help me to recognize the things that keep me from You and discard them. Slow me down and help me find the path to You. Amen

Lead me not into temptation — I can find it by myself.

JUNE 27

O Father, direct me to find the way to reach those that seek peace and relief from fear and anxiety. Show me how to be Your servant. Amen

The honeymoon is over when your wife complains about the noise you make when you are getting breakfast.

JULY 6

Father in Heaven, Your love for me is greater than I deserve. Help me to be worthy of Your love and to be the person You want me to be. Amen

An optimist is someone who tells you
to cheer up when things are
going his way.

JUNE 28

Dear Lord, today my self-esteem needs a boost. Since I am made in Your image, I need to love myself as I love You. Boost me up, Lord. Amen

The penalty for bigamy is two mothers-in-law.

JULY 5

Dear Lord, I know You are greater than my problems. When I am troubled let me not forget that I will find the strength I need from You. Amen

Age is not important unless
you're a cheese.

JUNE 29

Dear Lord, I know that pity will not feed the hungry, nor will prayers. Prod me to help the hungry today with food. Amen

The man who gets ahead is the one
who does more than is necessary.

JULY 4

Father, You have given me a sense of right and wrong. If I make choices that I know will not please You, give me the courage to admit my mistakes. Amen

Often the difference between a successful marriage and a mediocre one consists of leaving about three things a day unsaid.

JUNE 30

O Father, You enter my heart even when I am unaware of Your presence. Unbend me so that I will do Thy will with joy. Amen

With proper care, the human body will last a lifetime.

JULY 3

God is always with me. God bestows blessings of life, light and love on me and all His children. I have a special place in God's world. Amen

To err is human, to forgive, infrequent.

JULY 1

Precious Lord, today I will commend more and condemn less. Help me to refrain from judging others and keep me ever mindful of this promise all through this day. Amen

Always try to drive so that your license
will expire before you do.

JULY 2